3-11-60

5-31-60

LIFT UP YOUR HEARTS

WALTER RUSSELL BOWIE

Lift Up Your Hearts

ENLARGED
EDITION

New York   Nashville

ABINGDON PRESS

LIFT UP YOUR HEARTS

Library of Congress Catalog Card Number: 56-5370

B

SET UP, PRINTED, AND BOUND BY THE
PARTHENON PRESS, AT NASHVILLE,
TENNESSEE, UNITED STATES OF AMERICA

TO

ELISABETH

I pray not only that our Lord
May bless all that you think and do;
I praise Him with glad heart for what
He hath already wrought in you.

———————————

PREFACE

THERE are realities which do not change with the passing of time. Of such are the need of men for God, and the reaching up of their minds and hearts for God's answer to that need. So it is true that prayers which have been voiced in one period may have the same significance for times that follow.

The first edition of LIFT UP YOUR HEARTS appeared nearly seventeen years ago. In the Preface printed then were these words:

Some of the litanies and other forms of devotion which follow were written through recent years and used in the services of Grace Church, New York. But others of these, and nearly all the prayers for personal use, were written first for their inclusion in this book.

What I have desired to do can be set down in two sentences. In the first place, I have wanted these prayers and services to breathe the aspirations, hopes, and faith which are not of one time only, but are timeless. In the second place, I have wanted to express these in a form which would not fall short of the rhythm and music of the classic books of worship, but yet in words which are natural and congenial to men and women and boys and girls of our own century.

Since that time there have come from many quarters messages which indicated that the prayers then brought together have been a help in voicing some of the aspirations toward God which are in us all. Therefore, in response to those who have said they wanted it, this new edition of the book has been prepared. In it are the prayers and litanies and other brief forms of devotion which made up the original edition. These are rearranged under headings which may contribute to more convenient reference; and to them have been added, in this enlarged edition, a newly written litany and many prayers, and two hymns which in their spirit and form are prayers also.

The hymn "Lord Christ, when first thou cam'st to men" was written at the request of my friend, Dean F. W. Dwelly of Liverpool Cathedral, who wished to use it in the hymnal he was helping to compile, *Songs of Praise*, published by the Oxford University Press. Since then it has also been included in *The Hymnal* of the Protestant Episcopal Church and other hymnbooks. The hymn "Far, far away is Bethlehem" has appeared before in part, but it has been largely revised for inclusion here.

The title LIFT UP YOUR HEARTS is of course no newly fashioned form of words that belongs to a particular generation. It is the *Sursum Corda* of ancient forms of worship. The eternal impulse of all human souls is in this call. And the hope that goes forth with this book is that now anew, as in the generations past, the invitation "Lift up your hearts" may be followed by the living response, "We lift them up unto the Lord."

WALTER RUSSELL BOWIE

CONTENTS

11

LITANIES

SELECTIONS FOR
YOUNG PEOPLE

MEDITATIONS

A MORNING MEDITATION ON THE LORD'S PRAYER

Our Father, who art in heaven,

Help me to believe this day that there is a power to lift me up which is stronger than all the things that hold me down.

Hallowed be thy Name.

Help me to be sensitive to what is beautiful, and responsive to what is good, so that day by day I may grow more sure of the holiness of life in which I want to trust.

Thy kingdom come.

Help me to be quick to see, and ready to encourage, whatever brings the greater meaning of God into that which otherwise might be the common round of the uninspired day.

Thy will be done, On earth as it is in heaven.

Help me to believe that the ideals of the spirit are not a far-off dream, but a power to command my loyalty and direct my life here on our real earth.

GIVE us this day our daily bread.

Open the way for me to earn an honest living without anxiety; but let me never forget the needs of others, and make me want only that benefit for myself which will also be their gain.

AND forgive us our trespasses, As we forgive those who trespass against us.

Make me patient and sympathetic with the shortcomings of others, especially of those I love; and keep me sternly watchful only of my own. Let me never grow hard with the unconscious cruelty of those who measure themselves by mean standards, and so think they have excelled. Keep my eyes lifted to the highest, so that I may be humbled; and seeing the failures of others, be forgiving, because I know how much there is of which I need to be forgiven.

AND lead us not into temptation, But deliver us from evil.

14

Let me not go carelessly this day within the reach of any evil I cannot resist, but if in the path of duty I must go where temptation is, give me strength of spirit to meet it without fear.

For thine is the kingdom, and the power, and the glory, for ever and ever. *Amen.*

And so in my heart may I carry the knowledge that thy greatness is above me and around me, and that thy grace through Jesus Christ my Master is sufficient for all my needs. *Amen.*

A MORNING MEDITATION IN THE THOUGHT OF JESUS

O God, I go out today into a world where it is not easy always to remember thee.

But so did Jesus.

I shall be tempted to believe in the power of evil as stronger than the power of good.

But so was Jesus.

I shall walk in the midst of crowds to whom the reality of this world alone appears convincing.

But so did Jesus.

15

I may be disappointed in some whom I had thought that I could trust.

But so was Jesus.

Help me to remember him.

By his unshaken faith, make me keep faith.

By his unswerving righteousness, help me to keep trying to do right.

By his witness to the power of another world, keep me from worldly-mindedness, and set my affections on the highest things I know.

By his patience with those who disappointed him, make me be patient and forgiving, conscious of my own shortcomings, and most of all concerned that my Master need not be disappointed when he looks at me. *Amen.*

FOR MORNING, MIDDAY, AND EVENING

In the Morning

FATHER, with the waking day, our spirits wake to new gratitude for thine unfailing mercies, and we pray that with new strength we may serve thee in whatever work we shall be called this day to do; through Jesus Christ our Lord. *Amen.*

At Midday

O GOD, through whose good gifts our bodies are again refreshed, may the lifting up of our thought to thee refresh our souls with strength and purpose for the unfinished day. *Amen.*

At Evening

FATHER, as the day draws to its close, we thank thee for our goings out and our comings in, for work and rest, and for the blessings of home about us as we gather again for the food thy grace has given. Be with us in the evening and through the night, and help us to remember trustfully that the darkness and the light are both alike to thee; through Jesus Christ our Lord. *Amen.*

PRAYERS

FOR VARIED NEEDS

Thankfulness

O MY Father, before I ask thee for any new gift, I would bring thee a thankful heart for the blessings thou hast given:

> For my body rested by the night;
>
> For mind and spirit waking to another day;
>
> For the dear familiar things of home;
>
> For those I love, and for the love that comes to me beyond my own deserving;
>
> For life to live, and work to do.

Keep me from the ingratitude that would take thy continual gifts for granted, and help me to find instead in every experience of the day the width and depth of joy to which I may be alive; through him who brought the abundant life, my Saviour Jesus Christ. *Amen.*

Watchfulness

FATHER, as a new day comes to bring its unmarred opportunity, help me to use it better than I used yesterday. While yet there is time, I would remember the special temptations which have overcome me before, and can overcome me again unless I am better armed against them. I have been ashamed too late of the failures against which I ought to have been on guard. I have spoken harshly when I should have put a curb upon a hasty and bitter tongue; I have been so intent on my own way that I have turned others aside from the ways in which they might have walked more happily; I have been too pre-occupied to be understanding and to be kind. I do not ask that these faults may be forgiven now. I would not have the sharpness of my remembrance of them dulled. I ask rather that I may be made more thoughtful and more vigilant, so that when this day ends there may be less for which I need to be forgiven and more for which I may be glad, because I shall have tried to let the goodness of God express itself through my obedient mind and heart and will; through Jesus Christ my Lord. *Amen.*

The Spirit of Wonder

O GOD, who hast made this fair world and given it to all men richly to enjoy, help me never to grow dull to all its wonder. Because so many of its glories are familiar, let me not forget how wonderful they are. Keep my eyes open to the beauty of blue sky, to the changing pageant of the clouds, to the silver mystery of moonlight, and to the majesty of silent stars. May I feel in every sunrise a daily miracle of life and light renewed, and in every sunset a pledge of thine unfading light without which we cannot face the dark. So may no single day be common, but may each one bring the benediction of its immortal brightness to my soul; through Jesus Christ my Lord. *Amen.*

The Guidance of God

O GOD, if in the confusion of the day I forget thee, do thou in mercy remember me. Show me the way of righteousness now while the day is new, and let thy grace go with me so that I may not stumble nor stray; through Jesus Christ my Lord. *Amen.*

Humility

O GOD, our Father, since he who stands must take heed lest he fall, deliver me this day from the foolishness of pride. Grant that neither outwardly nor inwardly may I boast of my imagined powers. Give me such reverence for the real tasks of life that I may know that they are above my own unaided strength; that so with a clean mind and a pure heart I may turn to thee for the help by which alone I may stand unashamed when the day is done. And unto thee be the praise both now and ever. *Amen.*

Confession

O GOD, who hast promised forgiveness to the penitent, help me first to confess how much there is for which I need to be forgiven. Not only for wrongs I may have done, but more for the good I have left undone; not only for evil passions, but for emptiness of purpose, I bow before thy holiness, O Lord. What fullness of devotion have I given to him who died that I might be redeemed? What cross of service have I taken up and carried on a sacrificial way? What loads have I lifted from the shoulders of the over-burdened to take them on my own? Stir my heart, O Lord, to human sympathy before it is too late. Quicken my compassion for the hungry and the homeless, for prisoners and outcasts, and for all who are unfriended, lest at the Last Day I hear the judgment of Jesus, Inasmuch as you did it not to one of the least of these, you did it not to me. *Amen.*

Going to Work

O GOD, go with me as I go out into the confusion of the world. It is often hard to know the right; and even when I know it, still it may be hard to do it. I want to be faithful to the best that I believe in; but the best is high, and the common ways are easy. I need to be reminded of the way I want to go. Help me to keep a clean mind, a generous heart, and a courageous purpose. Let me never willingly bring harm to any man; and if in the complexities of things I cannot help, I do bring harm to any, keep me troubled and un-satisfied until I learn to make my good and his agree. When there seems to be no straight road forward, and I am caught in compromise, teach me to turn where there is least of evil and most promise of a future good. Let me not only pray, "Thy kingdom come," but do whatever one man can to let thy kingdom come through me. *Amen.*

God's Defense

O GOD, thou art my refuge and my fortress; in thee will I trust. Defend me from the perils that walk in the darkness, and from the temptations that beset me in the day. When my strength flags, be thou to me as the shadow of a great rock in a weary land. When my courage fails, hide me under the covert of thy wings. And when the shadows lengthen, give me light at eventide; through Jesus Christ my Lord. *Amen.*

The Realization of God

O GOD, I bring thee this one prayer. Show me thyself. Help me to know that I am not alone, but that with me is the Friend who will not fail. Make me quick to recognize the revelations of

thy presence which may come to me through
what I have thought were common things; and
whenever I behold thy purpose, help me to obey
it, so that I may learn to know thee better and
to love thee more; through Jesus Christ my
Lord. *Amen.*

The Stronghold of God

ALMIGHTY God, deliver me from the folly of
acting or thinking as though I must carry the
weight of the world. Not in my poor power but
in thine are the issues of life and destiny. Let me
trust in thy sure purpose, and be thou to me the
stronghold to which I may continually resort.
Preserve me from the fear of harm and failure
as I go out to meet what thou dost appoint for
me. And of thy mercy grant me a quiet mind
and an untroubled heart; through Jesus Christ,
who promised in thy name the peace that
passeth understanding. *Amen.*

Wholeness of Life

O GOD my Father, give me this day a healthy
body and a wholesome mind, a happy spirit and

a ready will to help wherever there is need; through Jesus Christ my Lord. *Amen.*

On Growing Old

O GOD, before whom my little span of years is like the brief shining of a candle, when the flame of this mortal life flickers and one day must go out, give me faith that beyond the shadows is thy eternal light. Create in me a deeper seriousness that yet needs not be sad. As I come nearer to the day when earthly possessions and pride must pass away, help me to seek more faithfully those inner riches of the soul which nothing can destroy. Increase my longing for life in God, and of thy mercy lead me on toward the beginning of its fulfillment now. Let me come unafraid toward the gate of death, with trust in the wonder that waits on the other side; through him who lived and died, and is alive forevermore, my Saviour Jesus Christ. *Amen.*

Courage

FATHER, who hast given us this new day, grant that, turning our backs upon the shadow of old

failures, we may turn our faces in new faith and
courage toward that brighter life on which the
light of thy redeeming purpose shines; through
Jesus Christ our Lord. *Amen.*

Dedication

O LORD, thou art our God: early will we seek
thee. Now in the morning, before the confusion
of the day begins, make our thoughts clear, our
hearts warm, and our wills ready to follow the
leading of thy will; through Jesus Christ our
Saviour. *Amen.*

Consecration

O LORD Jesus, who hast loved us and given thyself for us, grant that this day we may give all
that we have and all that we are in such honest
devotion to our several duties that thus in deed
and not in word alone we may show our thankfulness for thy redeeming love. *Amen.*

Direction

O HOLY Spirit, now in the clearness of the morning set the compass of our desires true, so that

through all the day we may keep our thoughts and actions in the straight course of thy redeeming purpose; through Jesus Christ our Lord. *Amen.*

Strength Renewed

EVERLASTING God, who hast promised that they who wait upon thee shall renew their strength, shall mount up with wings as eagles, shall run and not be weary, and shall walk and not faint: we pray thee for the wings of faith which rise above the dust, for the eager strength which is swift to dare, and above all for the courageous patience which can sustain us when the road is long and hard; through Jesus Christ our Lord. *Amen.*

Quietness

O THOU the Almighty and Eternal One, who hast said, Be still and know that I am God, let our hearts be to thee as quiet waters that even in their little depths can mirror the eternal stars; through Jesus Christ our Lord. *Amen.*

Sustenance

O GOD, who in all the ages hast nourished and sustained thy children, give us, we beseech thee, for our bodies such provision as their needs require, and for our souls the heavenly bread to strengthen us to serve thee all the days; through Jesus Christ our Lord. *Amen.*

A Joyous Spirit

O THOU who wast called the man of sorrows, and yet didst pray for thy disciples that they might have thy joy; grant us such sympathy as takes upon itself the burden of the sorrowing; and with it such glad courage as shall turn the way of sadness into the way of joy because we follow in thy footsteps, O blessed Master, Jesus Christ. *Amen.*

Quiet Confidence

O THOU who, before the mountains were brought forth or ever the earth and the sea were made, art God from everlasting, let the uncertainty of our souls be stayed on thine eternal strength. Give us such confidence in thy sustaining grace that no frailties of our own may make us afraid. In all things may we be faithful; and through all things help us to keep a clear conscience and a quiet heart; through Jesus Christ our Lord. *Amen.*

Light

O GOD, who hast promised that unto the upright there ariseth light in the darkness, grant to us such high purpose as shall lift our eyes above the clouds of error and the shadows of evil and enable us to see the beacons of thy guiding truth; through him who is the eternal light, our Saviour, Jesus Christ.

Against Anxiety

O GRACIOUS Lord, who hast watched over us through all our yesterdays, in thee is our peace for today and our reliance for tomorrow. As we remember the anxieties we need not have suffered and our dread of evils that never came, help us to commit ourselves more trustfully to thee. Lift us above our little fears to a steadier faith in thy goodness which does not fail; so that we may walk the changing roads of life with courage, knowing that thou wilt be with us all the way; through Jesus Christ our Lord. *Amen.*

Steadiness

GRANT, O Lord, that against the confusion of false choices and the restlessness of our unsure desires we may know that in thy will is our peace; through Jesus Christ our Lord. *Amen.*

A Happy Spirit

O GOD, who art the source of life and the fountain of all strength and joy, make us at one with the mighty forces which move through all created things. Thou who hast made our bodies art the same God who hast made the sun and stars, the wind and waters, the cloud-capped mountains and the fertile plains. Through thee the trees grow in the forest and the seed springs in the furrow at the touch of sunshine and of rain. So hast thou made us not for limitation but for happiness and health, that our confidence may be as the flight of birds and the lifting up of our hearts as the lark that soars and sings at dawn. Grant that we may enter into this our heritage of power and of gladness, and in body, mind, and spirit express the fullness of the life thou givest to those who look to thee; through Jesus Christ our Saviour. *Amen.*

Poise

ALMIGHTY and everlasting God, Lord of lords and Light of light, who art revealed in the unfathomable heavens and in the quiet of unhurried stars, let our restlessness find rest in thee. May our wills become obedient to thy greater will, so that we may move, as the stars move, in the orbit of eternity; and without confusion and without haste, but with shining steadfastness, go on our appointed ways; through Jesus Christ our Lord. *Amen.*

Light and Strength

O GOD, whose light is beyond our seeing, give us faith in thy guidance through the mystery of life. When disasters threaten, when death comes to those we love, and when disappointments shut us in, let us know that there is more to life than happiness. When the fogs are thick and the sea is troubled, strengthen us to launch out into the deep on what may be the way of duty; so that even when we cannot understand the mystery, we may win that mastery of life which is thy gift to steadfast souls, through Jesus Christ our Saviour. *Amen.*

A Peaceful Heart

O GOD, from whom the awful forces of the universe proceed, but at whose heart is peace ineffable, help us in the midst of action to find peace. Deliver us from shallow brawling and from unsure haste. Make our purpose so profound that all our powers may be as the flowing of great waters, too deep for noise, too strong to be turned aside. When obstacles confront us, may there be in us a quiet rallying of the force that shall break through; and when opportunities open, may we move forward with the sureness of the river that finds its destined channel to the sea. *Amen.*

Trustfulness

O FATHER, who givest both the sunlight and the rain, that the earth may be fertile and the grain may grow, we bless thee also for the changing weather of our souls. Thou givest alike the brightness of the days of joy and the clouded skies of disappointment. May we receive them both with trustful gratitude, desiring most of all that the seed of thy rich purpose may take root in us and grow; through Jesus Christ our Lord. *Amen.*

For All Conditions of Men

O GOD of manifold good gifts, deliver us from the narrowness of desiring that all should fit into the pattern native to ourselves. Keep us sensitive and understanding amid our differences, of youth and age, of taste and circumstance, of feeling and opinion. As we make excuses for ourselves, so may we be generous in our excuses for others; and by our remembrance that we are all one family in thee may we rejoice in that oneness which is deeper than the little things that separate; through him whose love can bind us all together, our Master, Jesus Christ. *Amen.*

A Thanksgiving for Friendship

MOST loving God, who hast blessed us with friendships which grow more beautiful as the years go by, help us to find in them the assurance that love never dies and that he who loves has entered already into eternal life; through Jesus Christ our Lord. *Amen.*

A Thanksgiving for Life

O GOD, who hast made the world so beautiful and hast meant us to be happy in it, help us to go out to meet life this day with singing hearts. For all that thou hast given, for sleep and rest, for body and mind that wake refreshed with morning, for work to do and strength with which to do it, for the duties that call us out and for the welcome of home to call us back when the day is done, we thank thee, Lord. *Amen.*

Calmness

O GOD, who art a hiding-place from the wind and a shelter from the storm, help us to turn from the tumult and clamor of the world to the calm of thy great assurance; through Jesus Christ our Lord. *Amen.*

The Undergirding of God

O GOD, whose eternal might doth undergird our insufficiency, help us to trust in thee when we are shaken and uncertain. Take away our needless fears, lighten our confusions, and give us such strength as shall enable us to meet steadily whatever the day may hold; through the grace and power of thy Holy Spirit. *Amen.*

1110232

Holidays

O GOD of all life, who hast given us bodies as well as souls, as we thank thee for the strength to work, so we thank thee also when weeks of work are finished and a holiday begins. Send us out, we pray thee, to wholesome happiness. If we may go into thy great out-of-doors, among the mountains, along the rivers, or by the wind-blown sea, give us vigor to enjoy them all. May we feel upon our faces again the sun and rain, and see again—away from our shut-in places—

sunrise and sunset and the kindling of the stars. In the daytime make us eager to be active; and at night give us rest and the quiet miracle of re-cruited strength. Grant us simple pleasures, clean amusement, and minds refreshed. Then, in thy mercy, bring us back in safety, more fit to serve thee in the days to come. *Amen.*

On the Road

O GOD, who hast given us thy wide and wonder-ful earth, let thy grace go with us on its roads. Keep us from absorption in our own selves, from irritable haste, and from the reckless folly that can bring disaster. Make us considerate and courteous, that neither through what we do nor through what we leave undone shall we or others fail to come safely to our journeys' end. *Amen.*

IN TIMES OF DISTRESS

In Time of Sickness

O GOD my Father, hold me in thy keeping. Thou hast made my body and hast meant it to be whole. Be with me when I am bewildered by sickness and by pain. Let me trust the power of thy healing; and above all and through all let me trust thy love that does not fail. Give me back, I pray thee, health and vigor, that I may set my hands again with gladness to the unhindered tasks of life; but if this may not be, then teach me still to serve as best I can with bent or broken tools. May any suffering I must undergo teach me sympathy with all who suffer; and may every gift of life renewed send me forth with a thankful heart to greater consecration; through Jesus Christ my Lord. *Amen.*

For Sympathy

MERCIFUL Lord, who lovest all thy children and by thy love dost lift us up to thee, help me this day in all things to be loving. Where any are discouraged, let me bring them the friendship which may give them courage. Where any are sad, let me bring them sympathy. Where any are joyful, let me be a sharer in their joy. May my thought be understanding, my heart sensitive, and my speech gentle. Forbid that I

should willingly hurt anyone by deed or word;
and if in anything I have to speak rebukingly,
help me to do it with the straightforwardness
that leaves no rankling barb behind and with
the compassion that is healing. May the knowledge of my own shortcomings make me always
merciful; through Jesus Christ my Lord. *Amen.*

In Time of Great Grief

O LORD Jesus Christ, who by thy life hast made
us able to believe in a heavenly Father's love,
come close to us in our time of agony. Thou who
in Gethsemane didst pray to be delivered from
the cross, be near us when we must drink our
bitter cup of sorrow and of desolation. Thou
who in thine own dark hour criedst, *My God,
my God, why hast thou forsaken me?*—hear
our cry. Teach us that beyond every Gethsemane and every Calvary there waits a resurrection. Help us to trust when we cannot see; and
by the comradeship of thy victorious suffering
to know that love and life are everlasting and
that God's mercy does not fail. *Amen.*

In Time of Bereavement

O GOD our Father, we give thee back the precious one whom thou hast given us. Here upon this earth we shall not look upon *his* face again, but we believe that in thy world of light the faces of the redeemed are bright with the vision of thy glory. Because our human love has lost so much, we cannot help but suffer; but teach us more and more to feel the fellowship in spirit which we can never lose. As *he* goes before us on the ways of the immortal life, may nothing in our grieving give *him* pain. Grant that *he* may already know, and grant that we may learn, that since love is of God it cannot die, and that we who have loved one another shall find again in heaven all our love fulfilled. And this we ask in the name of him who died and rose again and lives and loves forever, Jesus Christ thy Son, our Lord. *Amen.*

IN THE FAMILY

A Prayer Before Marriage

O CHRIST, who wast bidden to the marriage feast in Cana of Galilee, come thou with us as bidden guest that thou mayest make our marriage a festival for our souls. Teach us to remember thy word, that God is love; and help us so to build our love on God in all high purpose and devotion that day by day love may be to us an open gateway into more abundant life. *Amen.*

A Prayer of Husband and Wife

O GOD, who out of all the world hast let us find one another and learn together the meaning of love, let us never fail to hold love precious. Let the flame of it never waver or grow dim, but burn in our hearts as an unchanging devotion and shine through our eyes in gentleness and understanding on which no shadow falls. As the road of life we walk together lengthens, forbid that the dust of it should ever drift into our souls. Help us to have the sense to climb high places of memory and of imagination, so that we may remember the beauty that lies behind us and believe in the beauty that lies before. Make us sure that romance does not depend on time or place, but that daily it may be renewed as we recognize those larger possibilities in one another which love itself creates. Teach us to remember the little courtesies, to be swift to speak the grateful and the happy word, to believe rejoicingly in each other's best, and to face all life bravely because we face it with united hearts. So may whatever spot of earth thou givest us to dwell in be as a garden in which all sweet and lovely things may grow; through Jesus Christ our Lord. *Amen.*

Of a Mother

MOST loving God, because there are those who look up to me, I would look up to thee. They trust me, and I need thy help that I may not fail their trust. They learn from me, and I need to be enlightened so that what they learn may be only what is right and true. They think that in my love they find their safety. But where can we be safe together but in thee? For all love is thy gift, since thou art love, and thou wilt help us as we try to live in thee. *Amen.*

Of a Father for His Son

O GOD, who art our Father, take my human fatherhood and bless it with thy Spirit. Let me not fail this little son of mine. Help me to know what thou wouldst make of him, and use me to help and bless him. Make me loving and understanding, cheerful and patient, and sensitive to all his needs, so that he may trust me enough to come close to me and let me come very close to him. Make me ashamed to demand of him what I do not demand of myself; but help me more and more to try to be the kind of man that he might pattern after. And this I ask in the name and by the grace of Christ. *Amen.*

Of Sponsors in Baptism

O GOD, help me to be faithful to my trust. Make me reverent before the soul of this little child. So far as I am able, let me help *him* to choose the best that life holds out to *him*. Make me a better Christian, so that I may encourage *him* to follow Christ. *Amen.*

Of Parents

O GOD, our Father, we pray for our children; and we bless thee for thy goodness in giving them to us. Enlighten our minds and purify our hearts that we may seek for them only what is best, and count nothing that we can give too great if their lives through us may be fulfilled. Deepen our love for one another, that so we may surround them with a love in which there is no fear. Help us to make our home a place where they can feel secure, so that they may go out from it with happy courage, and coming back to it find peace and rest and confidence renewed. Grant that we may lead them toward the highest that we know, and let us learn of Christ so that what we know may be worthy of their souls' needs. And in Christ's name we ask it. *Amen.*

Home

O god of all goodness and grace, bless this house and all who come within it. We thank thee for the mercies given us: for shelter and for warmth, for food to which we may sit down together, for the little familiar things around us that have grown dear, for happy goings out and comings in. Help us to make this house in every lovely way a home, where children may grow up in confidence, where all shall be knit together in mutual trust, and where the heavenly words shall be remembered, that he who is greatest is he that doth serve. Here may our friends find welcome, and here may there be such clean thoughts and warm affections as shall make us fit for the coming to us of the greatest Friend, our Master, Jesus Christ. *Amen.*

The Family

O GOD our Father, we thank thee for our home and for our family. Help us to live each day so that none may be ashamed or sorry. Keep us from being thoughtless or impatient, and from ever forgetting all that ought to make us grateful. May our hearts be happy, our thoughts kind, our words gentle, and our hands quick to help. So as we learn more and more to love one another, let us know thy love for us through Jesus Christ our Lord. *Amen.*

Grace at Meals

O GOD our Father, as we come together for the food thy love has given us, we remember Christ

44

who was known to his disciples in the breaking of bread. May he be with us, and may his spirit enter into all we say and do. *Amen.*

O GOD, who hast given us so much, we lift our hearts to thee in gratitude, and pray that thou wilt make us quick to share the best we have with those who are in need; through Jesus Christ our Lord. *Amen.*

FATHER, for these thy mercies, and for fellowship in them, we bless thee in Christ's name. *Amen.*

FATHER, we thank thee for the bread for our bodies, and we pray thee feed our spirits with the bread of life; through Jesus Christ our Lord. *Amen.*

FOR THE CHURCH AND THOSE WHO SERVE IT

Of Ministers

O CHRIST, my Master, let me keep very close to thee. When I am tempted to be undisciplined or self-indulgent, let me remember thy forty days of prayer and fasting. When the fires of my spirit burn low, let me remember thee continuing all night in prayer. When I flinch from hardship, let me go with thee to thy Gethsemane. When I am lonely, let me turn to thee, my risen Lord. Whatever the outer facts may be, grant me thy gift of inner joy; in thy name and through thy grace. *Amen.*

Of an Organist

O GOD, who hast made the morning stars to sing together, let our human music also be acceptable to thee. Take the love of beauty thou hast given, take my head and heart and hands, and use them for thy praise. Let me remember all the souls that hunger for something which no words can tell, and help me bring them inspiration; so that the burdens of the weary may be lightened, the sad be set to singing, and the secret hopes and faiths of faltering men and women lifted up on wings of heavenly flame; through Jesus Christ our Lord. *Amen.*

Of a Sexton

LORD, I thank thee that what I can take care of is nothing less than the House of God. Whenever I go into it, may I remember thee. Bless all the work of my hands, and may every least thing well done be to thee like worship offered there. As I do my best to make thy House a place where people want to come, let me be glad in the knowledge that I too am a minister of God; in the name of Jesus Christ. *Amen.*

Of Officers in the Church

GRANT, O God, that we who are called to any office in thy Church may behold it as the body of Christ. Help us to remember that its life depends not upon money or any material things, but upon thy Spirit. Use in its service whatever abilities we may possess, but first make our own selves fit to serve thee. May we be reverent and humble, open-minded and sensitive to thee through souls attuned to worship. In all that we plan and do may thy thought guide our thinking, and thy purpose purify our hearts; through Jesus Christ our Lord. *Amen.*

A Prayer for the Parish

O GOD our Father, we thank thee for life, for love, and for great purposes to which we may be loyal. Fill this parish, we pray thee, with the spirit of Jesus, that through him we may worship more joyously and work more faithfully, as disciples who would be worthy of his name. *Amen.*

For Missions

O GOD, who hast blessed us with the knowledge of the gospel of Christ, make us glad to give of ourselves and of our possessions to carry his gospel to peoples and nations who lack what we have had. Not unto us, O Lord, but unto thee be the glory and the praise for the light which has been kindled in our own land. Cleanse us from all false pride of race and blood, from self-complacency, and from indifference to the hunger of any human soul. Teach us that life can nowhere find fulfillment except in Christ, and that in our universal need of him we are one with all mankind. And this we ask in the name of him who died for the whole world, and who only in a world redeemed can manifest his risen life. *Amen.*

A Social Conscience

O MERCIFUL Father, we come to thee confessing the sins of our civilization, in which we all have shared. We have been so bent upon our selfish ends that we would not stop to have mercy. When we have seen those whom the injustices of the world have bruised and beaten, we have passed by on the other side. We have built round ourselves the walls of privilege, within which we might not hear the passion of exploited men, the weeping of women, the bitter cry of children robbed of happy youth. O God of truth, make us understand. O God of judgment, wake us to repentance. O God of mercy, make us fit to ask for thy forgiveness, before it is too late. *Amen.*

Sincerity in Worship

O FATHER, who hast taught us that he who loveth not his brother whom he hath seen can-not love God whom he hath not seen, forbid that we should come to thee with a dishonest worship. May what we pray be what we first have tried to practice. Before we ask for thy forgiveness, help us to be forgiving. Before we seek thy mercy, help us to be merciful. Before we say we love thee, let us try to see in other souls all that may be lovable; for we cannot find thee unless we find thee first in those for whom thy Son, our Saviour, lived and died. *Amen.*

FOR THE NATION AND THE WORLD

For the Nations

O GOD, whose righteousness is everlasting but whose love is everlasting too, have mercy upon the peoples who by their follies defy thy holy will. We confess the sins of the nations. We know that pride and arrogance and cruelty unrepented cannot escape their punishment. Yet in thy mercy thou art more ready to cleanse than to condemn. Let thy redemptive work begin in us. Deliver us from the hard ambitions which make us blind to the right desires of others, and from the self-absorption which so easily can grow into suspicion, hate, and violence. Make us mindful not only of our own need but of the needs of men and women everywhere. Beneath all differences of race or color or language, help us to see the same great human aspirations struggling to be satisfied, and let us feel ourselves part of the universal family of the children of God. So shall we be fit to desire and to call forth leaders among the nations who shall find the ways to peace; through Jesus Christ our Lord. *Amen.*

For Peace

O GOD of love and mercy, grant us peace. Cleanse from our own hearts the greed and envy, the harsh misunderstandings and ill will, which are the seeds of strife. Correct the pride and passion which may move us as members of the nations, and teach us instead the patience and compassion of Christ. Make us quick to welcome every adventure in co-operation between the peoples of the world, that so there may be woven the fabric of a common good too strong to be torn by the evil hands of war. In the time of opportunity, make us be diligent; and in the time of peril and darkness, let not our faith fail; through Jesus Christ our Lord. *Amen.*

For an End to War

O GOD our Father, to whom all souls belong, help us deeply to feel and to confess the sin and shame of war. By the love of Jesus crucified to save mankind, lift us above unthinking hate for any people. By the power of his judgment on all self-righteousness, purge us of the stubborn pride that would deny our own shortcomings. Before we impute evil, make us concerned to repent of what may be evil in ourselves. When provocations come, give us the understanding that can be patient. When we are tempted to think of those whose interests clash with ours as only aliens and enemies, help us to believe that underneath our differences are love of home and the same longings everywhere for life and peace and decent opportunity.

To all who are in authority give wise and understanding hearts, that they may desire and strive for a community of the peoples in which each nation can find its life fulfilled. Increase in them faith and hope and perseverance. And grant that among the multitudes no hasty passions may weaken the hands of the inspired few whose undismayed devotion is given to the building of a world in peace. All this we ask in the name of the Redeemer, Jesus Christ thy Son our Lord. *Amen.*

The Correction of Pride

O GOD of truth, without whom our world drifts into darkness, let thy light burn through all our falsehoods and evasions. Deliver us, and especially all the rulers of the nations, from the arrogance of earthly power. Help us to know that when we forget thee whatever we build is labor lost, that only in thy life is our enduring life, and only in thy will our peace; through Jesus Christ our Saviour. *Amen.*

FOR SPECIAL DAYS AND SEASONS

Sunday Morning

O GOD, as once again the first day of the week brings its message of Jesus risen from the dead,

may his Spirit rise again in me. I thank thee for
rest from work, and for quietness in which to
worship, for time to think and pray and to set
the compass of my soul afresh. Forgive me for
what may have been the faults and failures of
the week gone by; and grant that this day, in
the company of thy people, thy Holy Spirit may
give light and life for the days ahead. *Amen.*

In Church

O GOD, whose love embraces all thy sons and
daughters, bind into one fellowship all of us
who gather here. Make us sensitive to the needs
that are in all human hearts: for light in hours
of bewilderment, for comfort in disappointment
and in sorrow, for strength against temptation,
for purity of purpose, for the hallowing of all
life. Make us conscious also not only of those
whom our eyes can see, but of that unseen company of the faithful in other generations whose
witness is round us like the hovering of great
wings. Unite us with them in faith and in devotion, as members of that communion which is
beyond all time or place. Through hymns and
prayers and spoken word, may Christ be re-

vealed to us today, to save us from our sins, and to make us more truly his disciples; by his redeeming grace. *Amen.*

Weekdays

O MY Father, compassionate and patient, the things of the world may press upon me today. It may seem that I have not time to pray. But let me not lose the high desire that belonged to the hours when I tried to commune with thee. Be with me on the ways where I must walk, even when I do not remember that thou art there. In the name of Christ. *Amen.*

The End of the Year

O ETERNAL God, who hast taught us through the words of Jesus that there comes a moment when a door is shut, what can we ask of thee as we stand outside shut doors through which we shall not go? No penitence can change what now is past, no sharp contrition fill the lamps we let go out, no tardy awakening let us share in heavenly feasts to which we came too late. For our failures we ourselves cannot atone. Yet by thy mercy grant that in our remembrance of our failures and our sins we may turn in trust again to the one complete atonement, offered in him who lived and died for us, thy Son our Saviour Jesus Christ. *Amen.*

New Year's Day

FATHER, as the old year ends and a new year begins, forgive us for the failures of the vanished days, and bless us in whatever we have truly striven for in days that do not die. Keep us from vain regrets, and let us go forward in the light of the best that we have learned. Purge our hearts both of shallow self-confidence and of cowardly fears, so that we may know that without thee we can do nothing but that in thee all things are possible; through Jesus Christ our Lord. *Amen.*

Epiphany

ETERNAL God, who by the shining of a star didst lead the Wise Men on their way to Christ, grant that in the sky of our hearts the light of thy revelation may so clearly shine that our wills may follow ever in the way that leads to him who is the Saviour and Redeemer of all mankind. *Amen.*

Lent

O LORD our Master, who through the forty days didst forget the body because thy spirit wast caught up in God, teach us with whole hearts to seek the heavenly communion, so that, being delivered from subjection to the flesh, we may be released into the spiritual liberty that belongs to the children of God. In thine own name we ask it. *Amen.*

Palm Sunday

O GOD, whose dearly beloved Son was greeted by the crowd on Olivet with halleluiahs, but in that same week was mocked as he went lonely to the cross, forbid that our welcome to him should be in words alone. Help us, we beseech thee, to keep the road open for him into our hearts; and let him find there not another crucifixion, but love and loyalty in which his kingdom may be established evermore. *Amen.*

Holy Thursday

O MASTER of life, who didst gather thy disciples round thee in the Upper Room to give them there the sacrament of thy body and thy blood, take us also, unworthy as we are, into the fellowship of those who would follow thee. We acknowledge our shortcomings and our sins, our inconstant minds and hearts, and our slackness in devotion. But thou dost not forsake us even when we fail thee. Accept us not for what we are, but for what thou canst create in us, O Saviour who by thy sacrifice hast sealed us for thine own. *Amen.*

Good Friday

ALMIGHTY and most merciful Father, whose power is in love, we bless thee for thine infinite compassion to the sins of men in that thou didst give thy blessed Son Jesus Christ to take upon himself the sufferings of the cross. Make us ashamed of the sins in us which crucify his love afresh, and fill our hearts with thankfulness for the undeserved and everlasting grace by which we are redeemed, through him who is the Lord of life forever. *Amen.*

Easter

ALMIGHTY and everlasting God, who on Easter Day didst turn the despair of the disciples into triumph by the resurrection of Christ who had been crucified, give us faith to believe that every good which has seemed to be overcome by evil, and every love which has seemed to be buried in darkness and in death, shall rise again to life immortal; through the same Jesus Christ who lives with thee for evermore. *Amen.*

Ascension

O LORD Jesus, who didst carry thy humanity back into the Eternal, we bless thee because through thee we can believe that the love revealed in thy life among men has been from the beginning, and is for evermore, the heart of God. *Amen.*

Whitsunday

ALMIGHTY God, who at Pentecost didst pour thy Spirit upon the apostles, let the everlasting miracle of thine unmeasured gift be renewed in our own time. Grant that the heavenly fire may descend upon our hearts to give us courage, and that the winds of the Spirit may blow through us in kindling power, both now and evermore. *Amen.*

Trinity Sunday

O ETERNAL God, Father, Son, and Holy Spirit, grant that in the majesty of all creation we may behold thy power that upholds us, in the face of Jesus Christ thy love that seeks and saves us, and in new life within our souls thy Spirit kindling in us; that so even to our littleness thine infinite wonder may be revealed, O blessed Tri-une God. *Amen.*

All Saints' Day

O GOD, who hast revealed the beauty of thy Spirit in the faces of those who have looked up to thee, we bless thee for those in every genera-tion who have reflected here on earth the light of heaven. When we walk through the dust of the crowded ways of life, or linger in the shadows of our own shortcomings, may we catch from them the inspiration of a shining purpose

that shall lead us on their ascending road;
through Jesus Christ our Lord. *Amen.*

Advent

O LORD Jesus Christ, whose spirit now and for
ever comes to be our judge, look upon us, we
beseech thee, in mercy. Cleanse from our hearts
all desires which are not according to thy will,
strengthen in us whatever may be Christlike, and
help us find our gladness only in that which
draws us nearer thee. *Amen.*

Christmas

ALMIGHTY God, who through the glory which
began at Bethlehem hast shown us that in a human life thou canst reveal the fulness of thyself,
grant that in our lives the beauty of Christ may
again be born, so that all men may know the
everlasting miracle of his incarnation. *Amen.*

For the Spirit of Christmas

OUR Father, who hast given us Christmas as the
festival of great joy, grant us the spirit of clean

merriment, warm hearts for one another's happiness, and such enlargement of our lives in lovingkindness as shall make room among us now for him whose name makes this day beautiful, Jesus Christ, thy blessed Son, our Lord. *Amen.*

The Miracle of Bethlehem

O LOVE of God, draw back the bolts of my foolish proud contentment, and open the shut doors of my heart. Here in my soul, narrow and cold and unworthy though it be, repeat the spiritual miracle of Bethlehem. Let me feel that into my humanness the divine has entered, to save me from my sins, and to give me the blessedness of new life in Christ. *Amen.*

FAR, FAR AWAY IS BETHLEHEM

Far, far away is Bethlehem,
And years are long and dim
Since Mary held the Holy Child
And angels sang to him;
But still to hearts where faith and love
Make room for Christ in them,
He comes again, the Child from God,
To find his Bethlehem.

Across the sea is Galilee,
And paths that Jesus trod,
And hidden there are those high hills
Where he communed with God;
But on the common plains of life,
Along the ways of men,
The voice that once said "Follow me"
Speaks to our hearts again.

Gethsemane and Calvary,
And Christ upon his cross—

Did evil triumph then, and make
All faith a bitter loss?
No! for the love of him who died
Is mightier than our sins,
And for all those who turn to him
The pardoned life begins.

Oh, conquered cross and empty tomb!
Oh, Easter morn of joy
That brought again the risen Lord
Whom nothing can destroy!
O Master over death and time,
Reveal thyself, we pray;
And as before among thine own,
Come dwell with us today!

LORD CHRIST, WHEN FIRST THOU CAM'ST TO MEN

Lord Christ, when first thou cam'st to men,
Upon a cross they bound thee,
And mocked thy saving kingship then
By thorns with which they crowned thee:
  And still our wrongs may weave thee now
  New thorns to pierce that steady brow,
And robe of sorrow round thee.

Oh, awful love that found no room
In life where sin denied thee,
And, doomed to death, must bring to doom
The power that crucified thee,
    Till not a stone was left on stone,
    And all a nation's pride, o'erthrown,
Went down to dust beside thee!

New advent of the love of Christ,
Shall we again refuse thee,
Till in the night of hate and war
We perish as we lose thee?
    From old unfaith our souls release
    To seek the kingdom of thy peace
By which alone we choose thee.

O wounded hands of Jesus, build
In us thy new creation;
Our pride is dust, our vaunt is stilled,
We wait thy revelation:
    O love that triumphs over loss,
    We bring our hearts before thy cross,
To finish thy salvation.

DECLARATIONS OF
BELIEF AND FAITH

A DECLARATION OF BELIEF

I BELIEVE in God, the creator of heaven and of
earth, Lord of all power and might;
I believe in Jesus Christ, in whom the grace and
glory of God became incarnate;
I believe in the Holy Spirit, by whom the
heavenly flame is brought to human
souls;
I believe in the Oneness of Him who is made
manifest in all things great and good.
I acknowledge the law of God which is written in the majesty of suns and stars;
I acknowledge the truth of God within which
alone we can be free;
I acknowledge the love of God by which alone
we are redeemed;
I acknowledge the fellowship of all saints
Who learned of Christ and lived for Him,
Who carried in their hearts the flame of
consecration and of courage,

Who dared and endured and triumphed
even in defeat:

The evangelists, the apostles, and the
martyrs,

The singers of the triumph of the soul,

The lovers and the servants of mankind,

Who gave their lives, and in the giving
found all life fulfilled,

Who in their gentleness were great.

Through them and unto God I lift my soul in
thankfulness and in eternal praise.

Amen.

A DECLARATION OF FAITH,
AT CHRISTMAS TIME

I BELIEVE in Jesus Christ, and in the beauty of
the gospel that began in Bethlehem.

I believe in him whose spirit glorified a little
town;

Of whose coming only shepherds saw the
sign,

And for whom the crowded inn could find
no room.

I believe in him whom the kings of the earth
ignored

And the proud could never understand;
Whose paths were among the common people,
Whose welcome came from men of hungry
hearts.
I believe in him who proclaimed the love of
God to be invincible:
Whose cradle was a mother's arms,
Whose home in Nazareth had love for its only
wealth,
Who looked at men and made them see what
his love saw in them;
Who by his love brought sinners back to
purity,
And lifted human weakness up to meet the
strength of God.
I confess our everlasting need of God:
The need of forgiveness for our greed and
selfishness,
The need of life for empty souls,
The need of love for hearts grown cold.
I acknowledge the glory of all that is like Christ:
The steadfastness of friends,
The blessedness of homes,
The beauty of compassion,

The miracle of many hearts made kind at
   Christmas,
The courage of those who dare to resist all
   passion, hate, and war.
I believe that only by love expressed shall the
   earth at length be purified.
And I acknowledge in Christ
   A faith that sees beyond the partial fact,
   A trust in life redeemed that looks beyond
   our present evil;
And I pray that this redemption may begin in
   us who kneel and say together now—(*The
   Lord's Prayer*)

A SERVICE OF
MEDITATION AND RENEWAL

ORGAN PRELUDE

A PERIOD OF SILENT MEDITATION

THE Lord will command his loving kindness in the daytime, and in the night his song shall be with me, and I will make my prayer unto the God of my life.

He that dwelleth in the secret place of the Most High shall abide under the shadow of the Almighty. I will say of the Lord, He is my refuge, and my fortress: my God; in him will I trust.

It shall come to pass that at evening time it shall be light.

This is the message which we have heard of him, that God is light, and in him is no darkness at all.

THE LORD'S PRAYER, AND OTHER PRAYERS

HYMN, OR OTHER MUSIC

70

A READING FROM THE BIBLE

THE LITANY FOLLOWING:

O GOD most high, whose dwelling is the light of setting suns, whose glory shines beyond the farthest star,

Lift up our hearts to thee.

O God, so infinitely great that we thy children seem sometimes far off from thee,

Draw near to us, we pray.

O God, whose love exalts our littleness, whose gentleness doth make us great,

Come thou into our hearts this day.

FOR all this day has held of happiness,

We thank thee.

For the familiar mercies which too often we forget, for food and shelter, for health and strength, for sleep and waking, for rest at night, and for the renewal of the morning,

We thank thee.

For our homes, for friendships, and for the unspeakable blessings of love,

We thank thee.

For light-heartedness and laughter, for all clean amusement, for the glory of the out-of-doors, for the flowering of spring and summer, for the splendor of autumn, for winter snow, and hills, and sky.

We thank thee.

For all around us which is beautiful, and for every material blessing which protects the inner life,

We thank thee.

YET with our thankfulness, O God our Father, for all that thou hast given, we join our prayers that we may be brave enough to desire thy greater gifts.

We pray thee, not most of all that we may be sheltered, but that we may be strong; not that life may be always pleasant, but that we may be dependable; not that we may receive much, but that we may give more.

For the grace to walk with joyfulness on sunny roads; but also for the gallantry to go forward without flinching when the road is dark and hard,

We pray thee, O our Father.

For such desire to do well as shall make us grateful for appreciation, yet never dependent on any man's applause; for modesty in success and for steadfastness in defeat,

We pray thee, O our Father.

For the simplicity of spirit which is glad in all our blessings, yet for the unselfishness which cannot rest until it shares the best we have with those whose need is greater than our own,

We pray thee, O our Father.

For clear eyes to see the highest, for clean hearts to love it, and for steadfast wills to follow on its way,

We pray thee, O our Father.

AND this above all we pray:

Help us so to know Christ and his life that the same mind which was in him may be in us, and that we, like him, may be in the world and yet not of it.

Help us so to know Christ and the grandeur of his death that we may be strong to walk upon his way, even when it leads toward a cross.

Help us so to know Christ and the power of his resurrection that as he was raised from the

dead by the glory of the Father, so we also may walk in newness of life.

A MOMENT OF SILENCE

HYMN

THE ADDRESS

HYMN, OR OTHER MUSIC

THE FOLLOWING PRAYERS:

O GOD our Father, as the evening shadows fall, grant that in thy light we may see light. May the remembrance of thy steadfastness shine above us like the quiet stars; and may all the noise and fret of the day be stilled by the benediction of thy peace; through Jesus Christ our Lord. *Amen.*

AND unto thee, O Father, we commit not only ourselves but all those who are dear to us, wherever they may be. Grant to them rest, and protection from all dangers of the night. Forgive them and us for any failures of the day, and especially for any sins against love. Help us more and more to learn our need of one another, and above all our need of thee, O Love that wilt not let us go. *Amen.*

A FINAL MEDITATION

> *I bind unto myself today*
> > *The power of God to hold and lead,*
> *His eye to watch, his might to stay,*
> > *His ear to hearken to my need;*
> *The wisdom of my God to teach,*
> > *His hand to guide, his shield to ward;*
> *The word of God to give me speech,*
> > *His heavenly host to be my guard.*
>
> *Christ be with me, Christ within me,*
> > *Christ behind me, Christ before me,*
> *Christ beside me, Christ to win me,*
> > *Christ to comfort and restore me,*
> *Christ beneath me, Christ above me,*
> > *Christ in quiet, Christ in danger,*
> *Christ in hearts of all that love me,*
> > *Christ in mouth of friend and stranger.*

O LORD Jesus, revealer of the Father, speak to us again thy promise: Peace I leave with you, my peace I give unto you: not as the world giveth, give I unto you. Let not your heart be troubled, neither let it be afraid. *Amen.*

LITANIES

OF PRAISE

O GOD, whose glory is revealed in earth and heaven, in fields and mountains and in rivers running to the sea, in sky and cloud, in rain and sunlight, and in the shining of eternal stars.

Help us to know and love thee more.

O God, whose greatness stooped to touch our lowliness, whose love hath looked on us forever in the face of Jesus,

Help us to know and love thee more.

O God, who through the Holy Spirit dost enter even into our own hearts to make us the temples of thy presence,

Help us to know and love thee more.

FOR all thine unfailing mercies renewed with each new day,

We thank thee, O God.

For the morning light that wakens us, for work to do and strength with which to do it, for the energies of the noonday and for the quiet of the evening, for night and rest and sleep,

We thank thee.

For warmth of human fellowship, for the love of friends and of those most intimately dear, for the trustfulness of little children, for the weak who need us, and for the strong who give us of their strength,

We thank thee.

For all high examples of the good and great, for pioneers and prophets, for heroes of the spirit in the warfare against the world, for sinners repentant and for common men and women fashioned into saints, for all those who for conscience' sake have dared to suffer and to die.

We thank thee.

For the will in us to follow thee, for all right desires reaching toward expression, for joy when we are true to thee, and for cleansing sorrow when we fail,

We thank thee.

For struggle and success, for achievements won with honor, for lessons learned through disappointment, for days of happiness and for days of hardship, for the good things we gain and for all things which we are made courageous to give up,

We thank thee.

For life with all its manifoldness, for the stimulus of changing duties, and for thy light and love that do not change,

We thank thee, O God.

O BEAUTY of God that fills all life with beauty,

Open our eyes to see.

O truth of God in which all life must find its purpose,

Open our minds to understand.

O mercy of God, that seekest us with thy redemption,

Open our hearts that thou mayest enter in.

OF THE REMEMBRANCE OF JESUS

O LORD Jesus, who hast promised that where two or three are gathered together in thy name, there thou wilt be in the midst of them,

Come thou into our midst, we pray.

O thou who wast made man that thou might-
est bring the love of God to man:
Jesus with thine understanding eyes,
Jesus with thy friendly hands,
Jesus with thy great heart of compassion,
Come thou into our midst, we pray.
O Master of the souls that look to thee,
Thou bringer of the more abundant life,
Human companion and yet eternal Christ,
Strong Son of God and Saviour,
Come thou into our midst, we pray.

JESUS, who in Nazareth didst fill a little place
with glory,

Help us to love and follow thee.

Jesus, going forth into thy Father's world to
mark the beauty of the lilies, the miracle of the
growing seed, the nesting of birds, and all the
daily wonder of the earth and sky,

Help us to love and follow thee.

Jesus, bringing joy to the marriage feast of
Cana, and comfort where any mourned,

Jesus, lord of life, and revealer of the life
eternal,

Jesus, radiant with God, so that nowhere couldest thou be hid,

Help us to love and follow thee.

Jesus, who didst make the lame to walk, the deaf to hear, the blind to see,

Jesus, bringing release to the captives and liberty to them that had been bound,

Jesus, preaching the gospel to the poor, and proclaiming the kingdom of God,

Help us to love and follow thee.

Jesus, whose gentleness drew little children to thee,

Jesus, compassionate to the sinful and the sad,

Jesus, terrible to all evil, cleansing the temple, unafraid of any man,

Jesus, by whom the weak were strengthened, and the strong were turned into another way,

Help us to love and follow thee.

Jesus, made in all things like as we are, save without sin; tempted in the wilderness; wearied often; disappointed, tried, yet never overcome,

Help us to love and follow thee.

Jesus, setting thy face steadfastly toward

Jerusalem, passing through Gethsemane, walking the lonely way to Calvary,

Help us to love and follow thee.

Jesus, faithful unto death,
Jesus, crying, "It is finished!"
Jesus, rising immortal into life,
Help us to love and follow thee.

BY THE music of the angels at thy birth,

Fill us with thy Spirit.

By thy boyhood's eagerness to be about the Father's business,

Fill us with thy Spirit.

By the love that drew disciples unto thee,

Fill us with thy Spirit.

By the fullness of thy living and by thy fearless willingness to die,

Fill us with thy Spirit.

By thine agony in the garden,
By thy majestic courage on the cross,
By the radiant power of thy resurrection,
Fill us with thy Spirit.

JESUS, strong and sufficient, to the side of the weak;

Jesus, the stainless, across the path of those who would stain themselves with sin;

Jesus, the courageous, to the help of the discouraged;

Jesus, the merciful, to the release of the repentant;

Jesus, lord of life, to all who would learn of thee to live,

O Master, come!

Even so come, Lord Jesus!

OF THE KINGDOM OF GOD

Holy, holy, holy, Lord God Almighty, which was, and is, and is to come.

Blessing and honor and glory and power be unto him that sitteth upon the throne.

And unto our God, forever and ever.

The earth is the Lord's, and the fullness thereof:

The round world, and they that dwell therein,

For thine is the kingdom, and the power, and the glory,

Forever and ever, Amen.

O GOD, the heavens are thine and the earth is thine, and all our life belongs to thee: help us to employ it in thy service only.

Hear us and help us, we beseech thee, O Lord.

We pray thee:

That thy kingdom may come, and thy will be done on earth, as it is in heaven.

Hear us and help us, we beseech thee, O Lord.

That all injustice, violence, and oppression may give way to the coming of justice, mercy, and good will.

Hear us and help us, we beseech thee, O Lord.

That unemployment and confusion and needless poverty may vanish, as darkness vanishes before the day.

Hear us and help us, we beseech thee, O Lord.

That thou wilt teach us so to use the manifold resources of the earth that none may surfeit and none may be in want.

Hear us and help us, we beseech thee, O Lord.

That in all our business and industry, cooperation may take the place of conflict; and that men may find their brotherhood in work that serves the common good.

Hear us and help us, we beseech thee, O Lord.

That thou wilt send thy grace upon all physicians, nurses, and men of science who battle with sickness and disease, so that the frontiers of ignorance may be driven back and new secrets of healing may be brought to light.

Hear us and help us, we beseech thee, O Lord.

That thou wilt keep alive the holy fire within the hearts of all who dare to be the pioneers and prophets of unwelcome aspirations; and that thou wilt give to us, the people, a readier willingness to listen to the hard demands by which alone we may transcend the inequalities, the cruelties, and the evils which too long we have endured.

Hear us and help us, we beseech thee, O Lord.

That thou wilt everywhere restrain the folly, pride, and greed that lead to war, and wilt implant among all peoples a resolute purpose to seek agreement in the ways of peace.

Hear us and help us, we beseech thee, O Lord.

That thou wilt bless all agencies dedicated to mutual understanding and to concord.

Hear us and help us, we beseech thee, O Lord.

That thou wilt give to all in authority the wisdom to perceive thy truth and the will to follow where it leads.

Hear us and help us, we beseech thee, O Lord.

That thou wilt guard the conscience and the courage of all teachers, that neither by fear nor by favor may they be led to teach anything other than the truth.

Hear us and help us, we beseech thee, O Lord.

And especially we pray that thou wilt bless thy Church: fill it with a passion for righteousness, and a zeal to serve wherever there is need; guard it from apathy, from ignorance, and from the subtle temptation of surrender to the spirit of this world. Make it obedient to the Master, and ready like him to sacrifice to the uttermost for those who wait to be redeemed.

Hear us and help us, we beseech thee, O Lord.

O GOD of holiness,
   Fill us with a purpose that is holy.
   O God of light,
   In thy light may we see light.
   O God of love,

Help us to love the highest and obey it.

And unto thee be ascribed all might, majesty, dominion, and power, both now and evermore. *Amen.*

OF SOCIAL PENITENCE

O GOD, our Father, who hast made us thy human children as one family in thee, so that what concerns any must concern all, we confess the evils we have done and the good we have left undone. We have spent our strength too often upon the tower of Babel of our own pride, and have forgotten the city that hath the foundations, whose builder and maker is God. We have been guilty of selfishness and strife when we should have learned to build in brotherhood. We have been content that we ourselves should prosper though many might be poor, that a few should feast while multitudes were famished both in body and in soul. O thou who hast taught us that whatsoever we sow that shall we also reap, help us to repent, before thy judgment comes.

FOR the clouded eyes that see no further than our own advantage,

We confess our sin, O Lord.

For the dulled imagination that does not know what others suffer,

We confess our sin, O Lord.

For the willingness to profit by injustice which we have not striven to prevent,

We confess our sin, O Lord.

For the selfishness that is quick to gain and slow to give,

We confess our sin, O Lord.

For the unconcern that makes us cry, Am I my brother's keeper?

We confess our sin, O Lord.

BUT, O thou who art ever merciful, take away the evil of our conscious and unconscious wrongs, forgive us for our unfaithfulness to the vision of thy kingdom, and grant to us a better purpose for the days to come.

FROM acquiescence in old iniquities,

Save us, O Lord.

From indifference to the human cost of anything we covet,

Save us, O Lord.

From the greed that wastes the resources of this rich earth,

Save us, O Lord.

From the ignorance that wastes the lives of men and women through unemployment, poverty, and deprivation,

Save us, O Lord.

From the cruelty that exploits the needy and defenseless,

Save us, O Lord.

From the blasphemy against the Spirit that sells the bodies and souls of children to the golden idol of success,

Save us, O Lord.

From false leadership in business and in government, and above all from feebleness in the people that lets false leaders rise,

Save us, O Lord.

UNLESS the Lord build the house,
Their labor is but vain that build it.
Unless the Lord keep the city,
The watchman waketh but in vain.

But he that sitteth upon the throne said
  Behold, I make all things new.

EVEN so, O God, let thy redemptive purposes work through us to build a new and better order on this earth, for the blessing of thy people and the glory of thy name; through Jesus Christ our Lord. *Amen.*

OF NATIONAL THANKSGIVING

O ETERNAL God, ruler of all the earth, we bless thee for our country. Bountifully hast thou given to us, beyond all our deserving. Thou hast made us heirs of what the untold ages have created: the majesty of upthrust mountains, the green of wooded hills, the prairies rolling to their far horizons, the fertile valleys where the rivers run. All that we can accomplish rests on this which thou hast given. Hear us as we bring to thee the tribute of our grateful hearts.

FOR all the mighty width of land from bordering sea to sea,
  We thank thee, O Lord.

For endless fields where the grain harvests ripen, for orchards with their golden fruit,

We thank thee, O Lord.

For cattle in the meadows, for the wild things in the woods, for the fish in the ocean and lakes and mountain streams, for the homely creatures of the barnyard, and for the infinite beauty of winged birds,

We thank thee, O Lord.

For rich ores hidden in the hills, for coal and oil and iron, and for all the treasures of un-numbered mines,

We thank thee, O Lord.

For the strength and skill of all the multitude of toiling men on whom our life depends: on farms, in fishing fleets, in factories, and before the fires of furnaces and mills,

We thank thee, O Lord.

For the genius of inventors, for the imagina-tion of engineers, for the daring of those who have dreamed a mightier civilization and have fashioned their dreams in stone and steel,

We thank thee, O Lord.

For those who laid the railroads and launched

the ships, for those who have built the bridges and lifted the towers of cities to the sky,

We thank thee, O Lord.

For all the host of men and women who in industry, in commerce, and in communications hold the world together because they are dependable at their daily posts,

We thank thee, O Lord.

For all the servants of the mind, for scholars and teachers, for authors and artists, and for all poets in word or deed who reveal the wideness and wonder of the world,

We thank thee, O Lord.

YET we remember that as we have greatly received, so in the same measure we are responsible. Forbid that we should be recreant to our trust, or that the fire which has been passed on to us should perish. Help us to be worthy of our fathers, and of our fathers' God.

To ALL the high desires of the pioneers and prophets,

O God, help us to be faithful.

To their belief in the possibilities of common men,

Help us to be faithful.

To their passion for freedom and their readiness to live and die in its defense,

Help us to be faithful.

To their scorn of tyranny, and their trust in men to rule themselves,

Help us to be faithful.

To their vision of a human common-wealth in which the folk from many lands might share,

Help us to be faithful.

To their release from prejudice and passion of an old world and their will to build a new,

Help us to be faithful.

O GOD, our fathers trusted in thee

And were not confounded.

They lifted their faces to thee,

And were not ashamed.

So enlighten us, O Father, and lead us on thy redeeming way; through Jesus Christ our Lord. *Amen.*

OF DEDICATION

I saw a new heaven and a new earth: for the first heaven and the first earth were passed away.

And I heard the voice of many angels, crying:

Worthy is the Lamb that was slain to receive power, and riches, and wisdom, and strength,

And honor and glory and blessing.

Blessing and honor and glory and power be unto him that sitteth upon the throne,

And unto the Lamb for ever and ever.

And I saw the holy city, new Jerusalem, coming down from God out of heaven, saying, Behold, the Tabernacle of God is with men, and he will dwell with them, and they shall be his people.

And God himself shall be with them, and be their God.

And God shall wipe away all tears from their eyes; and there shall be no more death, neither sorrow, nor crying, neither shall there be any more pain,

For the former things are passed away.

And he that sat upon the throne said,
Behold I make all things new.

O GOD of all the agelong yesterdays and of the infinite tomorrows, give us new faith, new hope, new power.

Hear us, and help us, we beseech thee, O Lord.

O thou who when the earth was without form and void didst breathe thy Spirit through the darkness, come with thy new creation to the chaos of our present world.

Hear us, and help us, we beseech thee, O Lord.

O thou who didst touch the prophets' lips with fire, send us thy prophets for the days ahead.

Hear us, and help us, we beseech thee, O Lord.

O thou to whom the heroes and the martyrs lifted up their eyes, give us the courage of heroic purpose now.

Hear us, and help us, we beseech thee, O Lord.

O thou who from the ranks of common humankind hast taken men and women and refined them with the holy flame, so that in every age those whom the world accounted least have become great; grant to us, the people, responsiveness to noble leadership, and the will to follow it even upon difficult and costly ways.

Hear us, and help us, we beseech thee, O Lord.

And especially we pray thee for the Church: Grant that it may be worthy of the name of Jesus. Keep it from cowardice and compromise, and from the subtle corruption of falsely bought success. May it not be conformed to this world, but more and more transformed by the indwelling mind of Christ; until it shall become indeed the body through which his spirit is expressed.

Hear us, and help us, we beseech thee, O Lord.

FOR great visions dawning already in our world,

We thank thee.

For belief in human brotherhood and for the will to make it true,

We thank thee.

For all men and women who will follow that hope in spite of postponement, persecution, and pain,

We thank thee.

For the seers who go before the crowd and climb the hilltop while yet we grope within the valley,

We thank thee.

For those who have dared and endured and triumphed in the power of an endless life,

We thank thee.

For those who in the radiance of their living have brought into our world the witness of the higher world in which their souls have dwelt; for their humor and their gaiety; for the laughter that made them seem light-hearted, even when they bore the burdens of mankind; for their sympathy and their tenderness; for their compassion to the weak, and their challenge to the strong; for the joyous abundance of their self-giving; and for all their shining witness to their Master, Jesus Christ,

We thank thee, O holy, blessed, and glorious God.

O CHRIST, Revealer of the Father,

Reveal thyself in us.

O Christ, who didst illumine the darkness of men's despair,

Make us believe in light.

O Christ, who dared to seem defeated on the cross,

Make us believe in love.

O Christ, invincible in sacrifice, risen and immortal,

Make us believe in God triumphant in all life.

And unto God the Father, God the Son, and God the Holy Spirit, be ascribed all might, majesty, dominion, and power, both now and evermore. *Amen.*

A LITANY OF THE BEATITUDES

O GOD of all goodness and grace, we thank thee for the promises given us through him who came as the Incarnate Word:

Blessed are the poor in spirit, for theirs is the kingdom of heaven;

Blessed are they that mourn, for they shall be comforted;

Blessed are the meek, for they shall inherit the earth;

Blessed are they which do hunger and thirst after righteousness, for they shall be filled;

Blessed are the merciful, for they shall obtain mercy;

Blessed are the pure in heart, for they shall see God;

Blessed are the peacemakers, for they shall be called the children of God;

Blessed are they which are persecuted for righteousness' sake, for theirs is the kingdom of heaven.

WE confess the sins and the shortcomings that hold us back from the blessings thou wouldst bestow.

From shallow contentment, and from the pride that makes us rich in our own conceits,

O Lord, deliver us.

From the easy self-pleasing that would shut our ears to the sorrows of the world,

O Lord, deliver us.

From the self-assertion that has no grace of meekness,

O Lord, deliver us.

From lust for the things of earth that may corrupt the love of righteousness,

O Lord, deliver us.

From hardness of heart that holds no compassion for the needy and the distressed,

O Lord, deliver us.

From the divided purpose that gives no full devotion,

O Lord, deliver us.

From irritation and anger that destroy the peace that thou wouldst give,

O Lord, deliver us.

From the softness and self-pity that will not suffer for righteousness' sake,

O Lord, deliver us.

Thou who alone canst save us from the sins that stand between us and thy benediction, grant us, we beseech thee, the blessedness which is offered even to us the undeserving who trust the promise of thy Word.

For a teachable and humble spirit, quick to
see within us and around us the signs of the
kingdom of God,

We beseech thee, O Lord.

For a heart that mourns with those who suffer,
and for a conscience that takes upon itself the
burden of our human sins,

We beseech thee, O Lord.

For faith that the earth shall be inherited not
by the violent and cruel, but by those whom thy
gentleness makes great,

We beseech thee, O Lord.

For hunger and thirst after righteousness that
shall not cease until thy purpose in us is fulfilled.

We beseech thee, O Lord.

For the spirit of forgiveness and of mercy, as
we remember how great is the mercy that we
ourselves must ask of thee,

We beseech thee, O Lord.

For sincerity of desire, notwithstanding all
our imperfections, and for thy atoning love that
may grant us the vision of God which only the
pure in heart deserve,

We beseech thee, O Lord.

For patient understanding and for reconciling grace by which all men may learn to live as thy children in a world at peace,

We beseech thee, O Lord.

For the power that belonged to all thy saints and heroes who dared to be persecuted for righteousness' sake, and for a will in us that can be faithful to the end,

We beseech thee, O Lord.

And the grace of our Lord Jesus Christ, and the love of God, and the fellowship of the Holy Spirit be with us evermore. *Amen.*

SELECTIONS FOR
YOUNG PEOPLE

PRAYERS FOR EVERYDAY LIFE

"When Christ was born in Bethlehem"

When Christ was born in Bethlehem,
There in the little town,
No royal robe was made for him,
He wore no kingly crown.

And as a boy in Nazareth,
The town in which he grew
Was full of just the simple things
God gives to me and you.

He did not want gifts for himself,
Except what all could share;
He loved the sunlight and the rain
And all the bright blue air.

He loved the little happy things
That come with every day:

His mother's smile, his food to eat,
And fields where he could play.

But most he loved to be a friend
Of everyone he knew;
He saw the best in everyone
As God himself would do.

He grew to be a man, and still
He lived among the poor;
And everyone who needed help
Came knocking at his door.

Kings of the earth were proud and rich;
He smiled and passed them by.
A kingdom of another kind
He would build by and by.

By love he drew men's hearts to him,
Until at length they knew
That God had come to them in him
And they must love him too.

And so they said, and we would say,
"Lord Jesus, be our king,
For we would have our hearts obey
Thy love in everything."

Prayer of a Boy

O LORD Jesus, I am only a boy, but you were also once a boy, and yet you made everyone who knew you glad. You did not try to have your own way, but you were always quick to see what others wanted. You did not look about for some- one else to do hard things in place of you, but you were ready to do your own work and to help others too. You made people want to be good, because you were so happy being good. You made people think of God because you thought of him so much that you were different. You were true and brave and kind. Help me to try to be like you. That is my prayer. *Amen.*

Of a Child

O GOD, I know that you must love me, because you have given me so much. I thank you for everything, and especially for * . . . Help me to love everybody, and to be kind and good. *Amen.*

(* *Here may be named the people and the things which the child is most glad to think of.*)

A Thinking-Aloud of a Boy or Girl

O GOD, you are so great and I am so small, and there is so much about you that I do not understand. I cannot see you and I cannot hear you, and yet the grown-up people tell me you are everywhere. I wish I knew how that can be.

But then perhaps I understand, at least a little; for there are things I cannot see or hear and yet I know are real. I cannot see the wind, and yet I feel it on my face. I cannot tell what makes the light above my bed, but when I need it, it will shine. I do not know how music and voices and all sorts of things I like to listen to come out of what seems only empty air. I know that these things happen, and they make me glad. Is that the way you come, dear God? —in something which I feel, though I cannot explain it? When I am glad because I know my father and my mother love me, is it you who made them love? When I try harder because they trust me, is it you who made them trust? When I am happy because I have done something kind for someone, is it you who put that kind thought in my heart? Is it you who are in all the things I think are beautiful? If you are,

then I know that I can love you, and I want
to love you more and more. *Amen.*

A Prayer for a Loving Spirit

O GOD, you have given me so much that I do
not want to forget to be grateful. So many people have helped me that I want to help wherever I can. So many people have loved me long
before I even knew it that I want to be loving,
not only to those whom I love already but to
someone else for whom nobody cares. Help me
at least in some little way to be like Jesus, who
went about helping people not because of what
they deserved but because he was glad to let
God's goodness work through him. And this
I ask in his name and for his sake. *Amen.*

Sincerity as Christians

O GOD, make me the kind of Christian who really
tries to follow Christ. Let me keep my body
under the rule of my best spirit, so that I may
not do anything careless, unclean, or cruel. Help
me never to be afraid of anything except of
doing wrong. Make me truthful and brave,

gentle to those who are not as strong as I am, and friendly and helpful to everyone. So as I try to follow Christ, help me each day to grow a little more like him; and this I ask in his name. *Amen.*

The Companionship of Christ

LORD Jesus, through all this day let me remember you, so that it may be as though you were standing very near. Help me to understand what you would do and then try with all my might to do it. By myself, I cannot always tell which way is right; but if you will show me, I will try to follow in it. Thank you for listening; and I think you will answer what I pray. *Amen.*

Faithfulness

O LORD Jesus, help me to remember that when I was baptized, the cross was signed upon my forehead, and that I belong to the army of Christians everywhere. Make me a good soldier. Keep me brave and true, obedient to the best I know, and not afraid to stand alone. Be near me as my Captain, and let me be loyal, whatever comes. *Amen.*

Before a Game

O LORD, help us to play hard and to play clean, to keep our courage and to keep our tempers, to be fair to everyone and never to do anything dishonest or mean. May each one of us play not for his own credit, but for the fun of the game and the good of the team. If we win, help us not to bluster or brag; and if we lose, help us to be cheerful and friendly, so that victory may have as good a taste to the other side as we shall want it to have to us when our turn comes to win. *Amen.*

Before an Examination

O GOD, be with me today and help me to do my best. Give me a clear mind and an honest heart. If there are things I do not know, let me not be flustered or afraid, but use to the utmost what I do know. May everything in which I have worked hard stand by me now; and if in anything I must face the results of laziness, make me resolve to work better in the days ahead. Help me to express all I know; but whether I can do that or not, grant that I may have learned something that will last; through Jesus Christ my Master. *Amen.*

Before Confirmation

O GOD my Father, help me begin to be your grown-up *son.* I am glad for what I have been taught as a child, and glad that already in baptism I have been made a soldier and servant of Christ. Help me no longer like a child but like a *man* to give my heart to him. Let me follow him, my Master and my Lord, so faithfully that he may never have to be disappointed when he turns and looks at me. Grant this, I pray, not for my deserving but for Christ's sake. *Amen.*

Family Prayers

O LORD Jesus Christ, we remember that the first disciples heard you call and followed you when they had hardly begun to understand what following would mean. Help us not to wait for all our questions to be answered, but to obey you now as clearly as we can and trust in you each hour of the day for the increasing light which you will give to those who walk upon your way. *Amen.*

LORD JESUS, we come together in your name because we want to know you better, for if we know you better, we shall love you more, and loving you will help us be more like you in what we think and say and do. Come to us, then, and be very real and near, we pray. *Amen.*

O LORD Jesus, we kneel here together because we love one another and because we know that we shall love each other better if you will come among us and show us how beautiful love can be. You loved people so much that you always trusted them, and because you trusted them, they tried to be better than they had been before. Help us to love each other that same way today, for thy dear sake. *Amen.*

POEMS AND HYMNS

Grace at Meals

JESUS, as by food we grow
Each day stronger, make us know

110

We must very eager be
With new strength to live like thee.

A Hymn for the Out-of-Doors

For dawn above the shining hills,
For shout of day begun,
For all the joyous round of life
Till eve and set of sun:
For march of mighty stars above
Our sentinels, the trees,
We thank thee, Lord, whose glory shines
Into our souls through these.

O wide eyes of the quiet lake
That gaze into the sky,
Help us with souls serene and clear
To mirror things on high:
O murmur of the ancient pines,
Wise with the lore of years,
Sing now to us a peace more deep
Than human frets and fears.

Bright ways that run among the hills
Up to each sunny crest,

Show us the brighter ways that run
For souls that seek their best:
High mountains climbing to the blue
Where happy feet have trod,
From all the dusty ways of life,
Oh, lift us up to God!

Hymn for Choir-Boys

As in thy temple, Lord, our feet
Stand where others stood before,
And as again our lips repeat
Hymns of all the years of yore:
Oh, make us feel the mighty throng
Of those who all the ages long
With saints and heroes swell the song
Of thy worship evermore.

And to the message of thy truth
We afresh, O Lord, would bring
From out the glowing heart of youth
All our truest offering:
Not only what our words intone,
Not lightly from our lips alone,
But with the hearts which are thine own,
Teach us, Lord, thy praise to sing.

A LITANY OF PRAISE

O GOD our Father, we kneel to thank you for so much that makes us glad. Sometimes we forget how glad we ought to be; and sometimes when we are glad, we do not stop to say so. But we want to remember now, and to bring our happy thanks.

FOR the world that is so big and beautiful,

Dear God, we thank you.

For the sun that shines on us in the morning, and for the silver moon and the stars at night,

We thank you.

For the great blue ocean, and the long waves foaming on smooth sands,

We thank you.

For fields to play in and for rivers and lakes and streams that come down from the hills,

We thank you.

For woods and trees and grass and flowers, and for the birds that fly and sing,

We thank you.

For warm bright days of summer, and for the

sparkling cold of winter ice and snow,

We thank you.

For all the happy outdoor places where we play, and for the houses we come back to when we are tired at the end of day.

We thank you.

For the schools we go to, and for the friends who go there with us; for teachers who help us want to learn, and show us how,

We thank you.

For the books we like to read, and for all the other books which are waiting for us when we are big enough to understand,

We thank you.

But most of all for our homes, and for all the love that made them and that keeps them safe for us.

We thank you.

For fathers and mothers and brothers and sisters, and for all the others whose names we are saying over in our hearts,

We thank you.

For what we have learned of Jesus, and for his promise always to be with us as our greatest Friend,
We thank you.

BECAUSE so many have loved us,
Help us to be loving.

Because so many have been kind to us,
Help us to be kind.

Because the world is so beautiful,
Help us never to do anything to make it ugly.

Because life can be so lovely,
Help us to keep it sweet and true.

(*The Lord's Prayer*)

A LITANY OF CONFESSION

O GOD our Father, we want to remember Jesus. Especially we want to remember how he went into a quiet place to think and pray and choose what he would do. Help us to bring our minds and hearts, as he brought his, for you to see. We are not like him, who had nothing to be

115

ashamed of; but we want to be like him, as much
as we can. We are sorry for anything in us that
is wrong, and we pray for a blessing on everything in us that is good; for Jesus' sake. *Amen.*

IF WE are to do better today and tomorrow, we
need to be forgiven for the blunders we have
already made. And so, for all our faults we know
of, and for the mistakes we made because we
did not know,

We ask forgiveness.

For greediness or laziness, and for anything
that has kept our bodies from being at their best,

Forgive us, O God.

For not trying hard enough to find out what
was right, and for cowardice in standing up for
what we knew was right and true,

Forgive us.

For thinking so much about ourselves that
we did not think of others and of what we might
do for them,

Forgive us.

For trying to get the best things for ourselves

instead of being quick to see that others had their share,

Forgive us.

For the times when we have hurt anybody, and for the times when we have been too careless to be kind,

Forgive us.

For the hasty words our tongues have spoken, and for the helpful words we did not have the sense to say,

Forgive us.

For any unclean speech or cruel gossip, and for ever forgetting to repeat the lovely things which would have made somebody glad,

Forgive us.

For any lies we may have told, and for the other lies we helped to spread by keeping silence when the truth was twisted,

Forgive us.

For ever having bullied those who are not as big as we, or having part in making any boy or girl unhappy,

Forgive us.

For bad temper and gloominess, and for nursing our grievances when we ought to have gone ahead with cheerfulness again,

Forgive us.

For cheating or crookedness in work or play or sport, and for cutting corners to get the things we wanted,

Forgive us.

For the little rudenesses which have disappointed those who loved us, and for every chance we have lost to be courteous and kind,

Forgive us.

But we do not ask, dear God, to be forgiven only. We want to be better than we have been before.

We remember Jesus, who gave his body, mind, and soul for God to use.

Help us to try to be like him.

By his shining goodness, he can make us glad in being good.

Help us to follow him.

By his strength he can make us strong.

Help us to follow him.

118

By his bravery he can make us brave.
Help us to follow him.

By his truth he can keep us true.
Help us to follow him.

AND so, our Father, as we have asked for blessing in our worship, we ask again for blessing as we go away. Help us to remember all that we have prayed for, and to trust in you to answer all our prayers; for Jesus' sake. *Amen.*

INDEX OF OPENING PHRASES

121

122

SUBJECT INDEX